MAKE YOUR

YOUR

SCHOOL
AWESOME

JENNIFER VIAUD, ED.D.

© Jennifer Viaud, Ed.D.

ISBN: 978-1-09837-940-7

CONTENTS

About the Author

Jennifer Viaud immerses herself in all things that involve creativity. She enjoys abstract painting, various forms of writing, and building fun and loving school environments that positively impact teacher morale. Dr. Viaud began her career in education as a middle school teacher and is now a successful elementary school principal. She understands the importance of being part of a valued team. It is her passion to build environments in which staff feel loved, appreciated, and are motivated to come to work each day. As a proud product of the New Jersey Public School System, attending a traditional high school and vocational school, Jen had earned the reputation of being a somewhat unconventional student. She has been able to use her life experiences to enact positive change by transforming and challenging the traditional educational environment.

For more information and to sign up for inspiring content, visit http://makeyourschoolawesome.com along with premium video content, latest news, updates, and insider exclusives, plus awesome DIY ideas for your classroom and school!

Introduction

● ● ●

I have spent twenty years of my life employed in public schools teaching the next generation of young people who will one day lead our world. Having the opportunity to impart wisdom, skills, and knowledge to our youth is one of my proudest achievements to date. As a novice teacher, I was able to experience various school districts around New Jersey in the role of athletic coach and substitute teacher. The very first full-time job I obtained was that of an inclusion teacher, visiting several classrooms across many grade levels. Through the years, I became a middle school language arts / social studies teacher and earned tenure in two different school districts. Years later, I took the leap into school administration. I had long sought to reestablish and create a school building with positive teacher morale, deeply rooted in its caring and loving culture.

Through my experiences, I have worked in school buildings that were warm, inspiring, inviting, and positive. However, I have also experienced school buildings that were cold, isolating, uninviting, and borderline toxic. It struck me that as educators, we spend the bulk of our lives giving to others; hyper-focused on our students, their well-being, their success, and carefully monitoring interaction with their peers. We genuinely understand that student behaviors potentially set the tone for the classroom, grade level, or even the building. However, as the building's key role models (teachers and staff members), have we ever examined how the adults in the building carry themselves? How do our interactions with our peers affect our students? Have we ever thought about our behaviors, our contributions, or the vibe we indirectly create on a daily basis?

As a school leader, I understand taking the time to inspire, support, and encourage teachers is critical. You are setting the tone and contributing to a happy, healthy, and productive work environment for your staff. By investing time and effort in building staff morale will plant the seeds of success for your students, and they will blossom! Remember, kindness is contagious. A happy teacher is a motivated teacher, and when teachers are motivated, there is nothing they can't accomplish.

Readers, get ready to gain all the ideas and tools to... MAKE YOUR SCHOOL AWESOME!!!

How's Your Vibe?

● ● ●

Everything we do, we do for our students. Every teacher and administrator has one common goal: creating the ultimate learning environment for their learners. But what is the ultimate learning environment? Take a minute, close this book, and think to yourself.

> "IN ORDER TO CARRY A POSITIVE ACTION WE MUST DEVELOP HERE A POSITIVE VISION."
> DALAI LAMA

I'm sure many of you envisioned high-tech classrooms, state-of-the-art equipment, and some funky *Jetsons*-looking furniture. Sure, why not! But what if I told you one of the most influencing environmental factors in a school *is you* and *your* energy? Wow, imagine that! Regardless of whether you're a paraprofessional, educator, volunteer, staff member, or administrator, the way you carry yourself at school and the energy you exude impacts your co-workers and the learning environment as a whole. Administrators and lead teachers can influence staff the most by creating energy and tone within a department, grade level, or even an entire school. Be mindful that this energy could positively or negatively affect the building's overall climate.

Ask yourself, what is the vibe in your school? Better yet, take a close examination of a small group of coworkers you frequently mix with. What's the vibe in that tribe? Take some time and think. How would you rate your school or district's overall feeling or atmosphere? Imagine you are a brand-new substitute teacher in your school. You venture into the teachers' lounge; what do you see? What do you hear? As a new substitute teacher, you stroll into the main office to wait patiently for your schedule. What's the vibe like in there? How do you feel walking down the hallways? Are you welcomed with warm, authentic smiles from fellow staff members who are eager to assist you with any questions you might have? Ask yourself one important question from an outsider's perspective: *would you want to work here?*

Understanding Culture and Climate

● ● ●

No matter what school district or building you work in, each community and their respective schools have their own internal struggles. It's so interesting as we examine different demographics throughout our large clusters of distinctive school systems. Many teachers assume the grass is always greener on the other side. I can tell you from working in a wide range of districts in contrasting areas, in both rural and urban settings, buildings may look different from the street curb. Still, they share similar interior and structural challenges. While each encompasses its own unique problems, no facility operates perfectly, and there is always room for improvement and modifications. I promise you, there is no school or district out there that is a total utopia. Never believe the social media hype!

"ATTITUDE IS A LITTLE THING THAT MAKES A BIG DIFFERENCE."
WINSTON CHURCHILL

Often times at workshops, we are thrown terminologies intensely focused on culture and climate. More specifically, how to build upon your school's culture and climate. These two words are usually slapped together and commonly echoed throughout the professional development community. Many believe they are similar, but they perform differently: culture is how a building operates and functions based upon behavior, while climate is best described as how staff and students collectively feel. Culture is developed deriving from daily operations or events, while the climate is more like the building's universal temperature. It simply describes the comprehensive collections of emotions or the building's vibe. How would you describe the culture and climate in your building?

Why Having a Positive
Work Climate Is Important

● ● ●

L eave it to Google to make everyone else look bad regarding promoting lavishing perks while creating exceptional work environments for their employees. This billion-dollar company sets an extremely high bar when it comes to splurging on their staff. Many of you are probably reading this while sitting in your office or classroom, stuffing an expired Twix Bar from the only operational vending machine in the school, but let's take a closer look at how large corporations allocate and invest tremendous amounts of money explicitly earmarked to promote positive work environments.

It is not uncommon for large corporations to provide complimentary refreshments, occasional corporate lunches, and everyone's favorite, "casual Fridays," but companies like Google take it to a whole new level. Google's employees can feast throughout the day on assortments of delicious snacks from their micro kitchens to their endless supplies of free breakfast, lunch, and dinner in their cafe-like, in-house eateries. Like various organizations, they also have a gym, but with a twist. Their facilities have high-end, state-of-the-art workout equipment, and staff has limitless access to exercise. After a rigorous workout, many personnel take advantage of relaxing in several of their modern employee lounges equipped with futuristic furniture, outfitted with games. Who's down for a quick game of foosball? Hey, and don't forget about the occasional deep tissue massage. Don't worry; they may have these perks, but do they have the pleasure of shaping the minds of future leaders of the world like we do? Didn't think so. Don't quit your day job in education just yet.

"THE THING THAT LIES AT THE FOUNDATION OF POSITIVE CHANGE, THE WAY I SEE IT, IS SERVICE TO A FELLOW HUMAN BEING."
LEE IACOCCA

Have you ever heard the phrase, "happy employees, even happier customers"? In 2018 Entrepreneur.com broke down this exact concept in an article entitled, "Investing in Your Employees is the Best Decision You Could Ever Make." Utilizing data from a Gallup report called "State of the Global Workplace," it was revealed that around 85 percent of people employed worldwide are not happy at work. Yikes!

But is this statistic truly so shocking? Researchers believe that this mindset points to a tremendous amount of "lost productivity," estimating around $7 billion in global revenue squandered each year. To put this simply, when individuals are not happy to be at work, they just don't work to their full potential. Virgins Group CEO Josh Bayliss understands the importance of listening to his workers: "Customers come second, employees first. It's a philosophy that brings unexpected benefits for both the company and its clients!" He certainly understands the importance of employee motivation and its effect on the workplace.

How Does This Apply to Education?

"IF YOU SEE SOMEONE
WITHOUT A SMILE,
GIVE THEM ONE OF
YOURS."
DOLLY PARTON

I f anyone deserves a happy and healthy work environment, it's our AMAZING teachers. Many have endured years of pressure from top-down initiatives and constant alterations to curriculum and district restructuring. Several have experienced forever-shifting environments where leaders (school administrators) come and go often. Some schools, unfortunately, feel as if their buildings have an unstoppable revolving door. I'm sure you've heard many of these grievances throughout your career in education. In recent times teachers were under a tremendous amount of tension and pressure after educating students virtually (or hybrid) for over a year. Some parents created an extra level of stress due to being over-opinionated after witnessing the sacred interior of a classroom. Could you imagine the *joy* one feels when juggling the multi-faceted virtual teaching experience to only have an individual with zero educational background or training tell you precisely what you're doing wrong and how their way is *so much better*! Unfortunately, that was the reality for many teachers during the virtual format shift. If the pandemic taught us anything, it was the danger of having too many chefs in the kitchen. Teachers need to refocus, build back confidence, develop genuine team camaraderie, increase collaboration, and make teaching fun and enjoyable again.

Could This Work at School?

● ● ●

I know exactly what you're thinking: Schools barely have enough budgeted funds for students' school supplies. How in the world could we invest in fancy lounges and provide gourmet meals? The simple answer is that creating a happy and productive work environment takes mostly creativity and effort, not a tremendous amount of cash flow. Well, one thing is for sure: many teachers, PTA members, and school administrators have more creativity in their pinkies than most working professionals in million-dollar corporations. Give someone in education a case of cardboard paper towel tubes, a bottle of glitter, and just watch the magic unfold.

"PEOPLE RARELY SUCCEED UNLESS THEY HAVE FUN IN WHAT THEY ARE DOING."
DALE CARNEGIE

What exciting and creative ways can staff members engage in the school atmosphere to help raise morale? To be honest, teachers and paraprofessionals, just want to have fun. So, let's focus on appreciating staff and changing the sometimes mundane and dreary work environments. It is also noteworthy to understand the importance of supporting one another. This takes zero creativity, just simple effort, and genuine care. If you are a teacher, a building administrator, or even a superintendent, you must lead by example. Take the time to show sincere interest in your colleagues' efforts at school. For instance, make supportive posters and head to that pep rally. Sit in the front row at that school play, cheer for that colleague running their first marathon—who knows, maybe even have the students make t-shirts and encourage them on their last week of training. You need to show members within your building your advocacy both in and outside the workplace. Your work colleagues are simply an extended family. Think about it: they are similar to real families! You can't pick them; you are forced to spend a considerable amount of time with them, some can really get on your nerves, but at the end of the day, you cherish your time with your coworkers and rely heavily on them. So, remember to appreciate and value their efforts—they are your teammates! Their success is your success. More importantly, their success will equate to student achievement. A happy teacher is a productive teacher.

Happy Teachers = Productive Teachers

● ● ●

Ask yourself this: when a teacher pulls into the parking lot during the early morning, rushing into the building, are they running in filled with excitement to come to work? Do you or others have that large pit in your stomach full of anxiety, nerves, and dreariness about what the day may bring? If that is the case, staff and administration may need to examine the contributing factors prompting such emotions. If a majority of people feel this way during the school day, the building's operations should be evaluated. Appropriate adjustments will be needed to shift the mindset of staff to forge a more positive and productive workplace.

Understand that when people have fun and pleasurable work experiences, it leads to a contagious and optimistic vibe that multiplies throughout the workplace. Happy people attract other happy people. It's that simple! Productive people influence and create more productive individuals. Research shows that happy people produce more than unhappy personnel. Employees who are excited to go to work each day tend to have more motivation, less stress, enjoy what they do, demonstrate improved performance, and exhibit increased productivity.

"TALENT WINS GAMES, BUT TEAMWORK AND INTELLIGENCE WINS CHAMPIONSHIPS." MICHAEL JORDAN

It is vital to create an atmosphere at school that will improve one's emotions and create synergy. Why? Teamwork is a crucial element of success in many professions, but it's even more critical in the realm of education. We rely on one another to create an atmosphere of collaboration and teamwork, building creative lesson plans with the help of others, not to mention the expansion of the co-teaching model. Developing a happy, positive, and productive work environment will improve teambuilding and create trusting relationships that will promote a healthy and thriving school atmosphere.

A Glance in the Mirror

• • •

"YOU CAN'T LIVE A
PERFECT DAY UNTIL
YOU DO SOMETHING
FOR SOMEONE WHO
WILL NEVER BE ABLE
TO REPAY YOU."
JOHN WOODEN

et's have a moment of truth and do a mini self-reflection activity. Think about your role in your current school and within your school community. During your daily actions and interactions with students and fellow peers, are you perceived as optimistic, positive? Do you acknowledge the accomplishments of others? Do you frequently celebrate building- and grade-level achievements not attached to you? Do you smile when walking down the hallways? When faced with a task or challenge, are you negatively outspoken, or do you look for the solution? Are you a ray of sunshine or the storm itself? Come on! We all know who the pessimistic peeps are. No matter what profession, every office, school, or business organization has at least one! You know, the person that challenges everything in the staff meetings. The individual who goes out of their way to complain or point out issues with the presented information. I'm sure you're envisioning that person right about now. If you are not, maybe that person is you—just kidding, that type of person would never reach for a book like this, so I think you should be OK!

As I said, your energy is like a magnet. Not only will that energy attract similar energy, but it is also contagious. So spread positivity, love, admiration, and joy while at school. Make a personal and individual difference, and be the change. Your positive vibe will grow and create an uplifting culture and productive work environment for all. Having fun, enjoying the journey, and not getting caught up on the bumps along the way is vital. Below I will list some essential ideas and activities that will promote a happy and productive work environment no matter your role in the school. These are benefiting tips and principles that will foster positive building morale.

What's Your Vision?

● ● ●

What is your vision for this upcoming or current school year? It is crucial to have this conversation with your colleagues and staff members. What is your actual end goal? To build a happy and harmonious school? To contribute to a nurturing work environment in which all staff feel accepted and are excited to work? To create a relaxing atmosphere to encourage positivity and collaboration? Maybe your goal is all of the above.

"ONCE YOU REPLACE NEGATIVE THOUGHTS WITH POSITIVE ONES, YOU'LL START HAVING POSITIVE RESULTS."
WILLIE NELSON

One beneficial exercise is to openly discuss your school building's current climate and develop goals while creating "vision boards." Vision boards are handmade poster boards with pictures and cutouts of inspiring topics, quotations, and images that help motivate individuals. They're like giant collages of one's desires to help energize and keep individuals focused on accomplishing their goals. Ask yourself or your coworkers, what type of building do we want to create? Through these meaningful conversations, start to discuss exactly what that building environment would look like in real-time.

These visions can be individual classroom goals, health and wellness goals, or perhaps overall building goals. Vision boards are an excellent resource for teachers and staff to glance at regularly. They act as friendly reminders of their desires, dreams, and affirmations for a more productive, harmonious, and healthy work environment. Create time throughout the busy school year to allow teachers to have some creative fun developing these vision boards. Encourage your staff to proudly display them in their classrooms, or perhaps build a giant team board and showcase it in your teachers' lounge as a reminder of this new goal for positive change.

Materials

Large poster board, glue, postcards, markers, magazine clippings, inspirational images printed from the Internet, glitter, ribbon, pre-printed inspirational quotes.

Directions

1. First, have a clear vision.

2. Collect and cut out items that match your desires and school building goals.

3. Start to glue and create a collage of your inspirational items on your poster board.

4. Have fun and be creative!

5. Lastly, proudly display your vision board in an area you or your staff frequently visits. The vision board should act as a memento of your building's obtainable goals and manifestations. Dream it, see it, and make it a reality!

So You're the Principal/CSA

(Lucky You)

"FIRST RULE OF
LEADERSHIP:
EVERYTHING IS
YOUR FAULT."
A BUG'S LIFE

1. <u>Appreciate Others</u> — Show your authentic and genuine appreciation! I'm not talking about a box of joe every September, left in the teacher's lounge with a card. I'm talking about true and meaningful communication provided regularly to your staff about their many accomplishments throughout the year.

2. <u>Always be Honest and Fair to All Staff</u> — Be real, be sensitive, be kind-spirited, and transparent at all times. Your rules and expectations must be universal and not only for a select group!

3. <u>Lead by Example</u> — If you create a directive, you yourself must follow that same directive. All eyes are on you, whether you like it or not. Challenges are part of the job. It is important to address those challenges appropriately and calmly.

4. <u>Put Your Positive Pants On</u> —Wear a smile and do your best not to let things bother you while in the public eye. If you are visibly upset, it can negatively impact the day and permeate to those you come in contact with. Remember, the energy you give off is absorbed by others and indirectly sets the building's tone. Be mindful of your words, be intentional with your actions, and especially be careful with your reactions. All eyes are on you; make sure you radiate calmness and empathy whenever possible.

Believe it or not, your supportive and loving demeanor will likely be mimicked; after all, kindness is contagious. Be gracious and considerate daily; over time, the positive and loving energy will spread! Remember: There's always that *one*. You can be the most loving, reasonable, and supportive administrator in the district. You may even regularly provide and care for your staff, similar to the examples shared within this book, but there is always going to be that one person. No matter what you do, they will be miserable, find things they don't like, and challenge your positivity. You know who they are. Almost every school building has one, but do not let them get to you. Keep your chin up in the storm, and look for those rainbows after the clouds have cleared! Above all, do not let their actions influence how you treat other staff members.

5. <u>Remember the Influence You Have</u> — You are the heartbeat and pulse of your building! Your behaviors and the way you carry yourself speaks volumes and impacts others. Just think of yourself as the protective ozone layer of your tiny and incredible world. You have the power to keep the building at just the right temperature and energy balance. Make sure your staff is protected. The nature of your job occasionally makes you the bearer of bad news or unpopular directives. Handle these obstacles and heated moments with grace and prevent yourself and others from slowly melting under pressure. Brace yourself; things can heat up quickly!

6. <u>Don't Make Professional Development a Drag</u> — Think outside the box, mix things up, and be resourceful. Whatever you do, don't make PD a dreadful experience. Consider the concept "Learn to Earn." Provide meaningful incentives and offer rewards to teachers and staff that fulfill learning opportunities. Research the latest and greatest and provide them with strategies and tools to practice daily. Do your homework *thoroughly* and preview your professional development presenters.

7. <u>Make Sure Your Building is Decluttered and Clean</u> — Nothing will upset your staff more than a building that lacks sanitation. The physical work environment will significantly influence your colleagues' mindset. Ensure it has a positive impact by keeping your facility clean and decluttered at all times.

Hey Teacher, How's it Going?

(Important Tips To Remember)

1. <u>The Glass Is Half Full!</u> — It really is. No matter how rough, challenging, and outright draining a situation can be, you need to find the good, so dig deep. Every dilemma and conflict contains a lesson to be learned. Create an opportunity to unite others to solve and combat these challenges. Change that mindset now.

2. <u>Ask for Help</u> — We are strong and independent as they come. We are teachers! Understand that even the most organized and talented problem solvers need some assistance at times. Asking for help does not show weakness, quite the opposite, it shows strength. Do not be shy to ask fellow team members for a brainstorming session or ask for ideas, regardless of the number of years you have in service. Great solutions can be found everywhere and do not participate in the systemic pecking order.

3. <u>Do Not Contribute to Negative Conversations</u> — I know what you're thinking: what do I do when I'm trapped in the teacher's lounge? It is unfortunate that many of these gathering areas become a venting place for our more vocal and less favorable staff members. My advice? Simply don't fan the flames. When challenged, provide meaningful feedback and solutions, but stay far away from the venting station. Remember,

not only are you shaping the minds of your students, but you are also a role model for other teachers and staff.

High Fives to Our Volunteers

(5 Tips To Parents, PTA Members, and Volunteers)

● ● ●

"WELCOME TO
PARENTHOOD; I
HOPE YOU LIKE
DESTRUCTION AND
CHICKEN NUGGETS."
ANONYMOUS

1. <u>Things Have Changed</u> — Yes, you heard me. I don't care if you were just "class mom or dad" two years ago; things have changed. Many parents are so eager to assist and make schools and classroom parties the best ever, just like they did for their older children. Maybe they are even trying to recreate an exciting school experience they themselves once had. This is an admirable and common goal, but trying to replicate things without an open mind sometimes tends to rock the boat. Volunteers must fully understand that schools change, rules change, budgets change, and medical and environmental issues change. Class parents and volunteers must be open-minded when a teacher or administrator says no to their famous peanut butter fudge brownies and prepaid dunk tanks; I promise they are coming from a good place. So go with the flow!

2. <u>You are Not a Guest</u> — When you volunteer, you are there to work! Your mission is to supply services to other students, not just your child or their select group of friends. Most importantly, you are not there to chat it up with the teachers and engage in a personal conference atmosphere. You must keep it professional at all times and resist the urge to go off-topic or lose focus of your volunteer role.

3. <u>This Is a No-Fly Zone</u> — Leave your pilot's license at home. It is important to be part of the school's many functions and show your child you are a positive role model by contributing and volunteering. This is all true and wonderful, but you are there for *all* children. It is too common, especially on field trips and grade-level functions, that some parents struggle to limit their interactions with their own children. Remember to mix, move, and mingle. Give attention and provide help to all the students, not just your child.

4. <u>What Happens in Vegas Stays in Vegas</u> — It is safe to say that our teachers and staff have received tremendous training about the importance of students and building confidentiality. We serve many children each year, and a considerable portion of our students have special accommodations, Individualized Education Plans, and 504 Plans. This is clearly one of our most vulnerable populations. While school is a safe and welcoming environment for all to flourish, volunteers must understand that discussing a child or a child's personal matters outside of school is always prohibited. Please refrain from any type of gossip, regardless of what you feel or your anecdotal perception of what best practices are. If you are in a volunteer role and want to report a situation, contact the teacher and/or administrator immediately. Please do not blast your concerns about the school community on social media.

Are You Ready to Make School Fun?

● ● ●

There are innumerable fun activities you can do with your staff. The ideas are seriously endless. Much planning and effort will go into each year, and it is our job as lead teachers and school administrators to make every new school year unique and special. So get ready to plan! Here are some simple tips before implementing some morale-boosting activities and events for your building staff.

1. **Hold on to Your Party Pants —**

    Transforming your school into a happy and enjoyable workplace will take buy-in. This will be a change for many and a drastic, somewhat uncomfortable change for some. Take it slow, and don't overwhelm your staff and teachers with multiple ideas for fun activities. You may find that staff will lose interest or simply get overwhelmed by doing too much too fast.

2. **Make Nothing Mandatory —**

    Remember to give options. If people think it is mandatory to participate in an activity, they will stress out and consider it as added work. Please note that we are trying to make work *less* stressful and enjoyable. After a successful event, you may be surprised to find staff quickly change their tune and jump in on the next one. As the culture shifts, so does the mindset.

3. **Find Resources —**

You are not the CFO of Google. Schools do not have an outrageous budget dedicated to increasing morale and employee wellness. Everyone thoroughly understands the financial constraints in schools across the globe, so it is no big shocker that your business administrator has not provided you with a block grant dedicated to this admirable cause. You must be proactive and creative. Look to your PTA, local businesses, donations from parents, and fundraisers to assist you in your efforts. If your budget is tight, look for activities that fit your budget.

To Theme or Not to Theme

● ● ●

As a teacher, I always dreaded experiencing the same old thing! Really, in my first 15 years of education, I was stuck in a loop, and things repeated like the movie *Groundhog Day*. I knew exactly what to expect, what the bulletin boards would look like. I knew what my neighbors were going to do, how their classrooms would be decorated. Sadly, like clockwork, I grew to understand what October "student projects" would hang in the halls, and you guessed it - the same sequence continued each year! I'm definitely not clairvoyant, but teachers tend to get into a rhythm of developing and following patterns. No matter what district I was in, the patterns continued. It felt mundane, predictable, and rehearsed.

It wasn't until my first year as a principal that I developed the courage to promote change. Promoting positive school change sounds like a 101 class in any admin grad school program, but let me tell you, you will need ample courage to ask 50+ staff members to switch things up. Consider how sacred the laminating machine is in every school building. Why? Because teachers love to recycle and reuse, and laminating helps them do just that. Hint: the same old projects will be on display year after year in the same area of the school. Just remember, whatever you do, DO NOT BREAK THE LAMINATING MACHINE! For real, you will not survive.

In hopes of changing this, I chose a "theme" for the entire school year, "WE ARE *WILD* ABOUT LEARNING." Every activity, decoration, newsletter, party, dress-up occasion, and door-decorating contest had a jungle twist. This was perfect since I was working with elementary school-aged children. Before teachers arrived in late August, I modeled some fun ideas. Picking up a few items from the dollar store, colored construction paper, and balloons, the building was transformed into a magical jungle. The hallways were swarming with oversized jungle animals and leaves. Our teachers seriously went bananas! Throughout the school, we displayed "All About Me" posters that had been mailed to students and teachers to return at the start of the school year. Our "WILD" entryway was new, refreshing, and helped the whole staff and student body learn a little more about one another. It was indeed a unique and exciting way to kick off the school year.

I quickly realized that I had been lucky to have landed at a school with a tremendously talented and dedicated staff. My teachers were all rock stars who took this positive, creative, fun mindset and ran with it. Next, I sent out an email looking for volunteers to compete in a door decorating contest. I was shocked by the staff's level of design and artistry infused into our hallway door designs.

A small basket of "homeroom" essentials with a zebra-striped bow was awarded as a grand prize for best door decor! Incredibly, everyone participated, and the building was truly transformed! Our teachers had a blast while engaging in a healthy competition that promoted grade-level camaraderie. Staff members were gifted pom-poms and jungle-themed hats/scarfs on opening day. With loads of enthusiasm, we played music and danced along as our students entered the school for the new year. Students were thrilled to be greeted by a dance party, and when they saw how their school had been transformed, they too went bananas. Their faces were gleaming with excitement which reminded us why we do what we do. That energy, enthusiasm, and new school environment set a positive tone for the remainder of the school year.

Creating a school-wide theme each year is uplifting and engaging for staff and students alike. Theme ideas can shape creative lesson plans, inspire unique student-centered activities, encourage school-wide contests such as Halloween dress-up, and much more - the ideas are endless.

Building School Theme Ideas

1. _**Learning is Our Superpower**_ — Superheroes, Capes, First Responders, Character Education

2. _**Our School Rocks**_ — Concerts, Rock 'n Roll, Music Appreciation, Math in Music Theory

3. _**Around the World in 180 Days**_ — Different Countries, Understanding Geography, Cultural Celebrations, Olympics

4. _**Learning Through the Decades**_ — 20s, 50s, 60s, 80s, The Future

5. _**Lights Camera Learn**_ — Hollywood, Different Genres, Red Carpet Readers, Famous Writers

6. _**Step Right Up and READ**_ — Carnival, Prizes, Math with Carnival Games, Animals

7. _**School is a Splash**_ — Underwater Creatures, Schools of Fish, Under the Sea, Mermaids, Pirates, Ecosystems

8. _**We are ALL Masterpieces**_ — Art, Beautiful Colors, Famous Artwork/ Artists, Gallery Walks, Art Education

9. _**Let's Navigate Together and LEARN**_ — Sailing Ships, Nautical Terms, Geography, History

10. *Our School is OUT OF THIS WORLD* — Rocket Ships, Space Exploration, Science, Physics, Learning About the Solar System

11. *After the Storm, Look for the Rainbows* — Great for returning to a new year post-Covid.

There is No Greater Feeling in the World Than Being Appreciated

● ● ●

"GRATITUDE IS
THE WINE FOR
THE SOUL.
GO ON.
GET DRUNK."
RUMI

D o educators and staff members who feel appreciated, supported, and valued exhibit higher productivity rates than their under-appreciated counterparts? Absolutely! I am not going to waste your time with the statistics; however, existing research indicates that when employees do not feel appreciated, they simply do not produce to their fullest potential and report feeling unfulfilled in the workplace. I spent two years researching such concepts for my doctoral dissertation. I will save you hours of reading; in short, as a school leader, you **MUST** support and appreciate the efforts of your staff if you expect them to perform as educational rock stars! A supported staff is a positive and self-motivated group that will far exceed your expectations. Their efforts and enthusiasm will tremendously benefit your students.

Take out that red pen, circle March 1st on your calendars! Why? Because March 1st is National Employee Appreciation Day! It is an important reminder to understand why large corporations invest millions of dollars in developing environments in which employees feel valued and supported. When employees have positive work experiences and feel valued, it increases productivity among staff. It promotes higher autonomy, work ownership, and feelings of pride. When the positive brain chemicals are flowing, employee stress levels subside, and they experience overall improved health. Not to mention that employee sick days lessen when employers provide a loving and caring environment. Expressing gratitude to fellow staff members is essential in creating a healthy and happy, productive work environment.

Many schools celebrate teachers, especially during teacher appreciation week! However, you shouldn't need a Hallmark Holiday to recognize your staff! Schools need to establish a daily culture of gratitude. Employees should be encouraged to appreciate one another actively, regardless of their role or position within the school building. Employees need to feel special and must be acknowledged for their efforts. It's essential to know your staff/coworkers and understand their level of comfort in a public setting. Remember, showing gratitude does not always need to be a grand, elaborate party for an individual. Appreciation could be displayed in a note left in a mailbox or a cup of coffee delivered to their classroom. In fact, sometimes, the simplest form of expressing appreciation can go a long way.

Every staff is different, and each team is comprised of unique players that all have a specific function in the success of your building. Take the time to notice individual and group contributions and be sure to highlight their efforts. Maybe a teacher or staff member has exceptional attendance, has gone out of their way for a child or parent, or has provided valuable assistance to a fellow coworker. Recognize and acknowledge these wonderful people! Work hard to establish a positive work climate where staff feel comfortable showing support for one another regularly and building camaraderie, not competition. Expressing gratitude by developing a culture of appreciation is a natural process and is quite contagious. Modeling gratitude with your staff will eventually cause a ripple effect, and you will witness the positivity multiply throughout your building. When you make people feel good, they will want to do good and be inspired to share the same positive feelings. Put that energy in motion and watch the good vibes flow...

Create a Wellness Area to
Show Appreciation for Your Staff

● ● ●

Now more than ever, teachers need to relax, destress, and unwind. Teachers play a crucial role in fostering learning for their students and provide for their social and emotional well-being. Added stress can negatively impact the classroom environment. A healthy teacher is a happy and productive teacher. Create a safe place for staff to unwind and to get that much-needed mental break during the busy day.

Staff wellness should always be a priority regardless of the district. In addition to developing a staff wellness center, consider creating a staff-driven wellness team. Your teams can provide valuable resources for school personnel about nutrition, perhaps host a weight management incentive program, or even host a healthy fitness lifestyle competition throughout the year. You may encourage and create afterschool activities that introduce staff workouts such as Zumba or yoga. Your school nurse and counselors are great candidates to lead the charge in providing wellness and mindfulness resources. School buildings are filled with knowledgeable professionals, so utilize your in-house talent!

How to Build a Staff Wellness Center

1. Find a quiet and private location (Teachers sometimes need alone time and a place to disconnect and decompress).

2. Create a space that is relaxing and inviting! Use calming neutral colors to paint or accent the room.

3. Bring plants into the space to help create a fresh look. They help provide clean air and reduce stress and anxiety.

4. Bring Positivity! Hang inspiring quotations throughout this space.

5. Flexible and therapeutic seating is recommended. Provide comfy movable chairs throughout the space with possible dividers to supply privacy for coworkers in need. (bean bag chairs/bounce-ball chairs/wobble stools/traditional chairs) and consider using dividers to provide privacy for coworkers in need.

6. Just like a spa, utilize a mini speaker to play calming music in the background (soft natural sounds / classical music/ raindrops / forest sounds).

7. Stretching is great! In a small area, provide staff with a mini mat to encourage participants to lay down on or stretch out. Display beginner yoga posters demonstrating some stress-relieving poses (e.g., child's pose, sphinx pose, reclining twist).

8. Mindfulness activities are a perfect solution for an overwhelmed staff member. Provide mini desks with stations to allow staff to practice breathing, mandalas coloring activities, journal writing, soothing puzzles, play putty, or any activity that encourages winding down the mind.

9. Diffuse essential oils. By providing fresh organic scents throughout your space, these oils will promote wellness and aid in lowering anxiety. I highly recommend using lavender oil in this space.

10. Lighting: Based on your space and natural lighting availability, it is vital to create a tranquil environment. Bright lights can be overstimulating and may not be best for this area; utilizing twinkle lights and curtains may help create a Zen environment.

11. Bonus: If budgets permit or donations are plentiful, you could include some wish list items: Inversion table, massage chair, area for tea or lemon/cucumber water, professional meditation recordings with headphones, mini library with wellness books.

Teacher Incentive Vouchers That Cost Nothing

"THE BEST THINGS IN LIFE ARE FREE. THE SECOND BEST ARE VERY EXPENSIVE."
COCO CHANEL

- Free Class Coverage

- One Week VIP Parking (park in the principal's spot)

- Sleeping Beauty: Allow Staff to Enter the Building 30 Minutes Later than Normal Reporting Time

- Get Out of Lunch Duty Pass

- Get Your Classroom Painted Over the Summer (Color of Choice)

- Skip a Faculty Meeting Pass

- I Like You a Latte: The principal brings you a fresh cup of coffee in the morning and delivers it to your homeroom.

- Get out of Field Day Pass

- Dress-Down, Morale Up! Free Dress-Down Day

- Extended Lunch: staff member receives an extra 30 minutes of blissful relaxation

- Helping Hand: Receive a Support Staff Member or Paraprofessional for an Entire Extra Period

- Don't Sweat the Small Stuff. Allow a staff member to wear sweatpants for the day.

- Good Ol' Booby Prize: When you clean out that storage closet from the 1970s, save those one-of-a-kind artifacts. For example, I once stumbled upon a 1960s-ish health bulletin board set. It was still in its dilapidated box, and the images and the slogans were simply hysterical. I awarded it to my PE teacher. Boy, did we both get a good chuckle.

Some Fun Ideas on How to Celebrate Others at School

"WOULD I RATHER
BE FEARED OR
LOVED? EASY. BOTH.
I WANT PEOPLE
TO BE AFRAID OF
HOW MUCH THEY
LOVE ME."
MICHAEL SCOTT
THE OFFICE

Ideas for Principals

September Room Transformation Prize — During the summer months, create a flyer requesting teachers to participate in a room transformation contest. Have them submit before and after pictures and share them with the community through social media. This will encourage parents to help out or maybe even donate some items. By sharing these pictures, parents can appreciate how teachers transform empty plastic-covered rooms into creative magical learning spaces before the start of school. Build a beautiful teacher's basket as a prize and maybe even toss in a VIP Teacher parking pass for a week.

EggCellent Job — When I first became a principal, I purchased a mini omelet maker. After adding some cheese and arranging the meal on decorative plates from the dollar store, I would present it to a lucky staff member during homeroom who was doing an eggcellent job! Simple, inexpensive, and seriously hilarious. I would try to make these at least once a week if the schedule allowed.

Shout Outs — These can be included in the morning announcements, emails, newsletters, a note left in the teacher's lounge, pop-in high-five during class, even a sincere compliment to staff members as they walk by.

Food Cart — Who doesn't appreciate a delicious surprise snack? Refurbish a small rolling cart with some cheerful decor and fill it up with snacks (for example: chips, cookies, water bottles).

Coffee Bar — Wake up and smell the gratitude. Fill the teacher's lounge with some paper coffee cups with handwritten messages of appreciation written on them. Place them near the coffee pot with a bowl of donated coffee pods and stirrers.

Never Forget Your Administrative Assistants — These brave souls truly are the heart of your building. Make sure they feel valued and supported daily. As your school's nuclei, their vibrations can be felt across the hallways and out into the community. Make sure they are happy, feel excited, and are ambitious to come to work each day. One of my favorite days of the year to celebrate is "Administrative Professional Day." I always do something extra special for these dedicated office staff members, usually a grand surprise as they enter their offices in the AM. Historically, I have transformed their work areas into themed decor with balloons and thank you banners. My all-time favorite experience was for my administrative assistant named Sue. The goal was to make her feel like royalty. I transformed our central office into a London scene by placing a large cardboard Big Ben in the corner, British flags hung from the ceiling, inflated balloons, and a surprise crown on her desk. The entire staff played along while dressing as if they were attending a royal wedding, even wearing those timeless fascinator hats. My incredible music teacher excitedly dressed as Elton John, and many staff wore cutout masks of the Royal Family. This was hands down the best day ever! Nothing beats an entire staff joining together to show their appreciation for a fellow coworker.

Extra! Extra! Read ALL About It — Create an "Our Staff is Awesome" bulletin board in the lobby. Be genuine and heartfelt about placing messages throughout the year to highlight staff professional development accomplishments, achievements, and milestones. Again, these boards can be cleverly decorated and easily incorporated into any schoolwide theme.

Grow With Us — How about a miniature plant to thank your staff for their continued efforts to grow and shape the minds of many each year?

SWAP — Give a go-getter an extra prep. Nothing says thank you better than appreciating the energy and time someone has invested in a project. Cover that teacher's class and give them some extra needed time to reflect on how thankful you are for their efforts.

It's a Potty Party — Get some (washable) markers and write some inspiring quotations on the faculty restrooms' mirrors. Show them your care by putting together a small basket at the beginning of the year with some hand wipes, miniature combs, perfume, hand cream, tissues, and mints. Have some fun, and maybe even leave a little weekly comic strip or a popular comedic meme taped to the back of the door. Make it personal and show them how special they are.

Food — This is an easy one. We all love those admins who drop a box of donuts in the teacher's lounge, but don't be ordinary, be extraordinary! Remember, you need to show your gratitude by offering your time and creativity. For example: After state testing, how about serving some hotdogs in a few crockpots with a few bags of chips? Place a big banner on the wall that says: "Staff, You Hit It Out of the PARK!" You could even possibly toss in a fun baseball cap dress-down day.

Have Fun — Don't be a robot! We get it, you have multiple master's degrees and maybe even a doctorate, but you don't need to act like a walking thesaurus. Seriously, show some humor, warmth, and sincere feelings, especially at those faculty meetings. Remember to have fun! Theme your meetings. Don't be scared to add a little pizzazz to the itinerary. As a principal, I love to do raffles, host Easter egg hunts, create physical challenges, and hide items throughout the building. Whatever you choose, just mix it up and be spontaneous!

Be the Elephant — We regularly show acknowledgment to our teachers and direct affiliates, but we need to remember everyone! That includes our custodians, volunteers, retired staff, administrative assistants, cafeteria staff, and school safety team members, just to name a few. Get to know all of them and share their contributions and your admiration for their dedication to the school community.

Snack Cart, Anyone? — I always recommend sending out a food preference survey in early September to find out if anyone has an allergy, or if a group of teachers are sticking with a specific lifestyle diet such as Keto. Grab some construction paper and an old cafeteria cart and get crafty. Decorate your food cart with thank you signs or inspiring messages and fill it with some treats your staff will get excited about. The key, however, is that you must deliver these snacks in person! Maybe even change up the theme or decor based on the holidays. Just put your personal touch on it and let the teachers and staff truly know how much you value all they do. Visit those classrooms and hand out those delicious snacks.

Encourage Dress Up Days — These are almost as fun as dress-down days, but no, seriously, allow and encourage your staff to have fun and wear costumes. Let them dress up on the first day of school to incorporate your school's theme, declare a twin day, or a "dress like your favorite hero day." There's Halloween, of course, but themes like Cat in the Hat, 100th Day of School, and 80s spirit week work too; whatever you choose, encourage it and make it exciting. My favorite dress-ups are "secret staff dress-ups": pick a theme but don't tell the kids and watch them giggle and ponder about what all of you are. Remember to give out prizes, send shout-outs over the intercom, or simply have students vote for their favorite. Just remember to be involved and make it memorable.

Design on a Dime — Nothing shows appreciation more than some rolled-up sleeves and elbow grease. Paint, decorate, and explore options for creating that special workspace for your staff. You could paint the teacher's lounge, build a wellness area for your staff to relax, give the library a fresh coat of paint, or simply update your courtyard with some fall mums! Your efforts will not go unnoticed; make that building as special as your amazing teachers and staff.

Just Hide It — No, I'm not talking about your emotions after you get that second nasty parent phone call of the day; I mean a physical object. For example, print out a picture of your mascot and laminate the image! Take this image and hide it somewhere in the school. Be crafty and adventurous. Let your staff know that there's a prize at stake to whoever finds the mascot! Remember, you can change this up depending on the season. Hide the pumpkin, elf, shamrock—you get the idea. Maybe award the winning staff member with a nice non-alcoholic (wink wink) bottle of something delicious.

Be a Principal that Rocks — Play an uplifting or even a comedic music "clip" every Monday morning and/or Friday afternoons on your intercom. Have fun with your music selections to match the vibe of the holiday season.

Positive Visiting Notes — Principals are in and out of classrooms every day. Why not leave a little ray of sunshine behind? By creating a genuine handwritten note, you can show your appreciation or leave positive words of encouragement. A little message can go a long way.

Ideas for Teachers/Paraprofessionals

"WHAT I DON'T LIKE ABOUT OFFICE CHRISTMAS PARTIES IS LOOKING FOR A JOB THE NEXT DAY."
PHYLLIS DILLER

<u>Let's Eat</u> — Teamwork makes the dream work! Create teams each month to host a luncheon in the teacher's lounge. Hot soup bar in November, green bagels in March, maybe even build-your-own-sundae in June. Have fun, and make sure everyone contributes! This will build camaraderie and give everyone a day each month to look forward to.

<u>It's Celebration Time</u> — Somebody is getting married! Or having a big birthday, about to retire, or gain tenure. Let's celebrate their milestones and accomplishments; remember they are a part of our school family after all. Having a little bash is always appreciated but try to host these events during portions of pre-planned faculty meetings or during lunch hours. More staff members will participate and will be eager to attend.

<u>S.O.S.</u> — Save our ship? Possibly. Let's develop that nurturing culture of helping out others regularly. Make a bulletin board where teachers can post notes outlining personal requests on areas where they need help.

Compassionate staff and colleagues can take down the Post-its and offer their expertise. One of the most significant roadblocks for teachers is the fear of asking for help, but the practice should become the norm in any healthy building.

Appreciation Station — Make an anonymous shout-out bulletin board in the teacher's lounge and encourage staff to place little compliments about fellow staff members on it. Encourage staff to contribute regularly and spread their admiration and love for others.

Let It Shine — Many schools have sunshine clubs. If you are unfamiliar with the idea, this is when teachers annually collect small sums of money from all staff to contribute to future gifts. These gifts are often earmarked for retirements, weddings, and baby showers. Take this idea and expand on it. Request time from your administrators to meet with your sunshine team weekly or during monthly faculty meetings. Carve out time from your busy schedules, building morale in the workplace should be a top priority for everyone. Recruit team members that are passionate about building morale. Each month create morale-boosting activities and creations for your work family.

Kindness Ninja — At the beginning of the year, provide each staff with a random "secret" buddy to look out for. Encourage them to become a friend, a support pal, or simply pay it forward with an anonymous act of kindness from time to time.

Celebrate the Holidays — Some of the happiest and healthiest workplaces I have visited had one thing in common: they all gathered together outside of school to celebrate at one point in the year. Keep it effortless, relaxed, and fun. It can be as simple as a holiday party or an end-of-year bash! Ensure everyone is invited and no matter their time in the district. Every staff member must feel accepted and welcomed.

Celebrate Your PTA — Make a PTA Day. On this day, once a year, students in their homerooms or at lunchtime are encouraged to make heartfelt personalized cards for their building volunteers. Present these cards at your PTA meeting and watch their warm reactions!

Ideas for PTA/Family Members

"VOLUNTEERS DON'T GET PAID, NOT BECAUSE THEY'RE WORTHLESS, BUT BECAUSE THEY ARE PRICELESS."
SHERRY ANDERSON

<u>Roll Up Those Sleeves</u> — Nothing shows gratitude more than effort. Create a volunteer team to repaint an area within the school. Maybe construct an outdoor garden, exterior relaxation area, or an outdoor classroom for your teachers. Show your love for your school by supporting the staff who do so much for our children!

<u>The Wheels on the Bus</u> — Spread the love to everyone, and let's not forget those special service providers such as bus drivers. Thank them with cards, treats, and praise for going that extra mile each day for our students. Remember, they do haul the world's most precious cargo. Make sure your school doesn't leave them out of the festivities.

<u>Feeling Hot, Hot, Hot</u> — OK, I'll just come out and say it: field day is not for everyone. I know you're shocked! Some teachers simply dread field day. You were probably too focused on that super-soaked teacher who volunteers yearly and goes headfirst into that giant dunk tank of dirt, but did

you notice some of the other staff members melting in their one size fits all field day t-shirts? Teachers always put their best foot forward and slap on a great smile, but I promise you showing the staff some extra love and appreciation on this particular day will go a long way. Save some of those teacher's appreciation supplies for late May and June. Possibly supply them with some cool refreshments or a mini fan and provide pop-up tents for extra shade.

Build a Welcome Wagon — Think outside the box! Yes, I'm sure you will go bonkers with teacher appreciation week. It is beyond appreciated and greatly looked forward to each year. Now, let's focus on expanding that base on the sometimes-forgotten staff who especially tend to have lower retention ratios. These staff members are much needed and relied on to have a properly functioning school. New staff and substitute teachers often disappear in the busy surroundings and tend to become camouflaged with all day-to-day activities. Make them feel respected and valued! Possibly provide them a little school booster club kit, invite them to a PTA/PTO meeting, order them school spirit t-shirts, or maybe send them a shout-out at a school-sponsored sporting event. Let them know they are at a solicitous school and part of the winning team.

Support the Cause — There are tons of morale-building activities that the teachers and administrators can provide for the staff throughout the year. Many of these activities are super exciting to participate in and sometimes even warrant some good old competition! Help them out and take up a gift card collection to be used as prizes throughout the year.

Front Line Heroes — Every school has a nurse or two. Some even have class-ranking security officers, try not to clump them into the traditional teacher appreciation festivities, make an effort to recognize their extraordinary commitment to school safety separately.

Sip Sip Hooray — Cheers to that special building admin team or principal. Strangely enough, these individuals often go unnoticed throughout the chaos. Although they are always on the move and look involved in everything, it is quite a lonely job. Once a year, highlight their efforts and show them that the community appreciates everything they do, maybe even bringing them a cup of joe! (Depending on how their year is going, perhaps they would even enjoy a different type of beverage.)

How About Those
Epic Faculty Meetings?

● ● ●

Raise your hand if you are thrilled or even a little excited to attend your school's faculty meetings. Don't worry—I'm sure everyone reading this has two hands firmly planted on this page. It is an unfortunate reality that many faculty meetings are boring, dreaded, and even (sometimes) a quasi-waste of time.

As a school leader, it is essential to bring substance and productivity to these meetings. They should focus on district initiatives, developing committees to succeed in school goals, and providing teachers with community learning time to maximize student achievement in their classrooms. Overall, I'm sure many school leaders have found ways to etch out itineraries focused on these essential components. Luckily, these meetings in the past few years have evolved.

"I CAN'T WAIT FOR TOMORROW'S FACULTY MEETING." SAID NO TEACHER EVER

Even while we have witnessed this evolution, such productive meetings have added work to sometimes long and stressful days. An educator's day is action-packed, to say the least, and a lengthy meeting at the end of it is not something they look forward to. Faculty meetings are essential for the success and growth of any thriving school. Still, we must be mindful while crafting detailed meeting agendas, and understand that teachers will most likely have a hard time absorbing all this information at the tail end of a long workday. We must work towards making this experience less exhausting.

How can we make faculty meetings better? Well, we need to flip the script! Many administrators simply continue to use the same monotonous tone of their predecessors or mimic the traditional meeting environments they themselves were subjected to as teachers. The most valuable element to educators is their time. If an agenda can be created and distributed prior to the meeting, you can easily communicate valuable topics and group tasks ahead of time.

It's also important to give your hardworking educators some time to wind down! Jumping into the agenda right after school can be mentally draining. Many teachers haven't even processed that their day has just ended. Start your meeting with some excitement; give them time to reflect, giggle, or even relax. Change the pace of their day for the better.

Meeting Icebreakers

● ● ●

Like any great stand-up comedian, the principal and/or presenter should never provide new material to a cold audience. Yikes! It's a daunting experience to see time ticking by as multiple people you are presenting to wear the same blank stare, obviously having a hundred other things on their minds. They chat, fidget, or simply drift away mentally. Wake them up, get them engaged, and have some fun with them. After reading the room or understanding the vibe through the week, you may choose to start off the meeting with a fun activity such as an icebreaker or a physical challenge. These are great for workshops, faculty meetings, or PTA meetings.

Icebreaker Warm-up Activities

The School Historian — Every school has one! Nothing breaks the ice like a team bonding by reminiscing about years past. Place staff in groups and space them out. They must have enough space so each group can whisper without being overheard by another. We don't like it when savvy teams cheat (wink-wink)!

So here are the rules: Once teams are adequately separated, provide each with an extra-large paper sheet and a marker. Now you begin reading out interesting and possibly humorous questions about the school's history or some fun facts about the staff. For example: Name the last five superintendents. What was our school's original mascot? List the three newest teachers to join our staff.

Remember to do your homework and ask veteran staff members to find those perfect questions. Also, humor is great, but be mindful of your questions; you don't want to upset any staff. I would stay far away from age or career longevity questions because this could be a sensitive topic. Make the game enjoyable. After reading 10-12 questions out loud, have teams hold up their answer sheets for review. The team with the most correct answers wins the game.

Rain Jacket Game — The rain jacket game is a fun icebreaker that will get every staff member on their feet. At the beginning of your meeting, place a stack of large flip chart papers in the center of the room. Ask each faculty member to take one sheet of paper. Direct them to fold the paper twice and tear one corner, thus creating a circular hole in the center of the paper once it's unfolded (demonstrate this step yourself). Have each staff member wear their "rain jacket" by placing their head through the center circle. Done correctly, each staff member will be wearing their paper poncho with room to write on all sides. Pass out bright-colored markers to each faculty member and encourage them to walk around the room. Ask everyone to scribe a message of appreciation on each other's back. At the end of this exercise, invite everyone back to their seats.

Allow them to take off their rain jackets simultaneously and take in all the beautiful messages, and kind words of appreciation fellow staff have written about them! Staff members can keep these papers for those rainy days when they could use some encouragement or appreciation.

Junkyard Swap — This is kind of hilarious, so get ready. It is also recommended to do this activity around the holidays because gift wrap is so abundant! Place a large square of gift wrap in each staff's mailbox. Leave a note asking them to participate by wrapping a small item and bringing it to the meeting (creative gifts and practical jokes are welcome). Place staff in medium to large groups at each of the tables. All the groups will need a set of dice. Each staff member will start with a random gift in their hand, so have everyone at the tables mix up their gifts. Write the following directions about the dice's numeric values on a large sheet of paper and put it at the front of the meeting room:

1. — Everyone switches their gift right.

2. — Everyone switches their gift left.

3. — Dice roller may steal any gift.

4. — Dice roller may steal any gift.

5. — Unwrap your gift. You're stuck with it.

6. — Unwrap your gift. You're stuck with it.

Play this game until everyone has an unwrapped gift that they cannot trade again. This activity is humorous, and staff will easily unwind as they participate.

Snowball Fight — Save this one for those crisp winter days. Create teams of five. Hand each team sheets of lined white paper. Ask each teammate to jot down a "fun fact" about themselves that no one would guess. For example: "I have climbed to the top of Mount Vesuvius." Once each team has their fun facts completed, have them crinkle up the paper, creating a "snowball." Ask the groups to throw the balls towards you, making the visual ambiance of a snowball fight! As you randomly scoop up snowballs from the floor, read the fun facts aloud to the groups and allow all of the teachers in the room to try to guess which team/ person they belong to! This can be hilarious, and the staff can learn a little more about one another! This activity is excellent for the long winter months. Feel free to pair it with some hot cocoa in the back of the meeting room for some added cheer!

Treasure Hunt — Take a large bag of chocolate or candy and hide it in your building or meeting room. On each table, place a simple photocopy of any crossword puzzle. You can find these on the internet or even in a local newspaper. Make it simple! On each copy, circle the boxes containing the letters that spell out the location. Divide staff up into teams sitting at each table. Teams have to work together in a timely fashion to fill out the crossword puzzle, locate the highlighted letters, then unscramble the words at the bottom to spell out the location. The team that completes this first will dash off to uncover the hidden prize! I recommend getting a big bag of candy so they can share it with the whole room. Such a fun and sweet way to kick off any meeting!

Roll the Dice and Break the Ice — Put faculty members into groups of five to eight. Using a piece of paper numbered 1 through 12, write unique questions or incomplete statements such as: "What's your favorite song?" or "The craziest thing I ever did was…" or "One thing that made me laugh out loud in school was…" Think outside the box when creating these questions. You can customize them to fit the interests of your faculty or school district. Place each piece of paper in the center of the table with a pair of dice for each group. Take the first five minutes of your meeting and give your teams time to chat, roll the dice, answer the questions the dice number lands on, and get to know one another a little more.

Fishbowl Fun — I recommend placing a large bag of Goldfish crackers on your presenting table as a prize, just for some visual motivation and excitement! Assign teachers to teams of 5–8 (smaller groups work best). Distribute miniature pre-cut pieces of paper to each team while holding a fishbowl in your hand. Explain to the staff that they are important role models who inspire students each day. Now ask them to think of some influential people in history, from George Washington to Aretha Franklin. Encourage them to use their imagination! Tell staff members to write down a celebrity or famous person's name on the paper, but not show it to their teammates. Instead, ask them to fold the paper and place it in the fishbowl.

Once you have collected all the papers, shake the bowl and mix up the folded pieces. Distribute a folded paper to each team member in the room.

It's now time to play a little Taboo/Charades. Each team member must read the paper and, without saying the name, act out or describe the person. The team that successfully guesses the name on each piece of paper in their group wins the bag of goldfish! This is a timed game, so circulate around the room and make sure everyone's having fun!

Left, Right, Center — This is becoming a popular game throughout homes in the US. The LRC game is simple, quick, and easy to learn. This game is great for groups larger than three and consists of chips and three dice with the letters L, R, and C inscribed on them. Creating teams of around 5–8 allows this activity to take up minimal time, making it a great icebreaking activity to kick off any meeting. I recommend pre-creating a few treat bags that you can award to the winner at each table when the activity is completed. If you don't want to make it yourself, LRC game kits are inexpensive and can be purchased at local stores or online. I highly recommend jotting down the rules on a piece of poster paper to hang at the front of the room to assist you when explaining the directions. This game might be an excellent wish item for you to ask your PTA to donate to your school in September.

Who's Smarter Than a Fifth Grader? — We know the honest answer: no one…these kiddos know everything! This faculty meeting warm-up activity is super quick and a great way to kick off any meeting when the bulk of the time is needed to accomplish agenda goals. Even so, it will get everyone shouting and quite possibly laughing out loud.

Create flashcards with simple, elementary questions. For example, "Who was the third president of the United States?" "Who is SpongeBob's best friend?" or "How many elements are on the periodic table?" Make them fun, and don't forget to add in some relevant pop culture questions to keep everyone's interest! Grab a large bag of Smarties and toss them to the teachers who shout the correct answers. I would go through a quick 15–20 questions, and once everyone is awake, the meeting can start.

Team-Building Activities
(Physical Challenges)

● ● ●

How great would it be if we could construct a giant octagon in the faculty room, UFC style, so everyone could hash out their differences and burn off some steam? I know we have all imagined doing that from time to time. Unfortunately, we have OSHA and unions, so we will just have to stick to old-fashioned hands-on team-building activities to get the blood pumping. It's nice to change the mood on special occasions and introduce physical team-building activities to the staff meeting agenda. These are not your routine meeting warmups, but they are indeed entertaining and competitive! Such activities are exciting and fun, but just like delicious chocolate, remember that they are best used in moderation. Don't include these physical activities *too* much because they will become chores rather than something your staff looks forward to participating in.

Okay, so where do we start? The first one I'm going to introduce on this list is a wonderful way to kick off the new school year. It will take a tremendous amount of time to complete, but it's a great way to introduce new staff, build camaraderie, mix new groups of teachers, and shake things up. The remainder of activities could be used to start or end any meeting.

Did Someone Say Scavenger Hunt?

● ● ●

Think *The Amazing Race*, but so much cooler! Let your staff know it's vital to understand the community they serve, so why not get out and see the area firsthand? Start out by creating teams of four. You may choose to make some smaller teams, but this hunt will need to hit the road, so make sure they can fit in a traditional-sized vehicle. Prior to the "hunt," you may want to encourage your teams to create a name, make team t-shirts, and who knows, maybe even flaunt a flag with their team logo on it! Build up this competition and get the community involved. I suggest making a trophy and involving key community members throughout the scavenger hunt to make this event extra special. Provide each team with a list of 10–15 items they will need to take a team picture in front of (minus one team member taking the photo, naturally). Each list should be identical, and the first team who arrives back at school with the completed photos wins!

Helpful hints: Make the list items and locations in different orders, so you don't have everyone headed in droves to the same place at the same time—yikes!

Some items may include:

1. Take a photo with your mayor (Town Hall)

2. Find your school's mascot

3. Stop monkeying around—team photo at the playground

4. Local town park (picture of a plaque or tree)

5. PTA president's house

6. Favorite local coffee shop

7. A fast team is a winning team—picture at the track

8. Local celebrity (find that special person and get them involved, maybe a retired teacher, former police chief, favorite parent, or community member—every town has one)

9. Lucky to work with this bunch—picture in front of a lotto jackpot sign

10. Our team is SUPER! Snap a shot in front of the superintendent's office

If road trips are not your jam, this scavenger hunt experience can just be as spectacular inside your school. You have the option to keep this party inside or simply limit it to your school's grounds. This can be an exciting way for new staff to learn key elements and essential locations within your building. A fun idea would be to print out large school logos or large pictures of your school's mascot and place them in prime areas: classrooms, child study team offices, and most importantly, the faculty lounge vending machine! Have fun and think outside of the box. You can step it up a notch by strategically hiding the logos to make the search even more exciting.

Why Team-Building Activities?

● ● ●

I t is paramount to understand why effective leaders invest their time and energy in team-building activities. Staff must support one another and stand as one. Creating strong bonds between educators and among staff members only increases productivity. One of the most significant elements in education is that teachers successfully collaborate and generate cohesive teaching methods. A school's environment is forever changing. New teachers come and go each year due to pupil population and staffing needs; teachers, CST members, and paraprofessionals continuously shift to different assignments, departments, and sometimes buildings to fulfill district needs. Regardless of the district's size, it is infrequent to experience some change from year to year. Due to this ongoing phenomenon, it is crucial that building leaders invest time for teachers to build camaraderie and forge healthy working relationships as new teams and staff evolve.

Generating time for team-building activities can increase a team's problem-solving skills, help develop creativity, and allow staff to uncover their colleagues' strengths and wisdom. Team-building activities help educators bond, work through disagreements, increase communication skills, and encourage motivation. These activities may feel slightly awkward when they are newly introduced, but they will become a positive norm over time. By promoting teamwork, they will help foster building morale, which is crucial in the most healthy and productive work environment.

Physical Challenges

I can't help but think of Oliva Newton John's song "Let's get physical"! Your staff needs to move around, but sweatbands or PE clothes aren't required just yet. If your teachers need to blow off steam or could use some energetic team-building activities, why not dedicate time to physical challenges? These are a great way to have your teachers and/or staff compete in physical obstacles to help change any dreary school day's tempo. These mini competitions can be action-packed and comedic at times. Make them fun and simple, and always be prepared prior to introducing them. Make sure you create enough copies of directions and purchase all supplies ahead of time. I highly recommend having the meeting area set up before staff arrival. Just like when you are teaching, downtime for participants is counterproductive and can dampen the mood. A good meeting facilitator is a prepared one!

"FIND A GROUP OF PEOPLE WHO CHALLENGE AND INSPIRE YOU, SPEND A LOT OF TIME WITH THEM, AND IT WILL CHANGE YOUR LIFE."
AMY POEHLER

Suppose these kinds of activities are your fancy and you feel that your staff could benefit from regularly participating in physical challenges.

In that case, I recommend creating and continuously updating a leader-board—a place to display which teams take home the gold throughout the school year. Maybe share your activities and winners in a tweet, weekly newsletters, or dedicate a building bulletin board to show your students how cool their teachers and staff members are after the bell. How neat would it be to give a trophy to the team that has won most often at your end-of-year assembly? Just a thought: remember that we must celebrate others' accomplishments as effective leaders. Check out some of these potential physical challenges you can do with your staff.

Many of these are similar to the team-building activities you've experienced at camp growing up, one-minute challenges you've seen on social media platforms, or games you've played at parties with your friends. Why are they worth trying? Physical challenges and competitive activities can enhance group engagement. They can change the meeting tone while getting the blood flowing. Take a look at the descriptions and materials, and choose the type of physical challenges that will best fit your staff's needs.

Change, Anyone? — Be the change you want to see in the world! Gandhi has inspired all of us; we are working in education, after all. The game works as follows: Divide your staff up into teams. Then choose one or two team members at a time and place them at different tables. If you have teammates from the same team at one table, they may sit across from their partner. Try to avoid sitting them next to each other—this could be problematic once the game begins, as the loose change could spread out too easily. Place a large pile of pennies in front of each person and blindfold them. Using only one (1) hand, each person must create the tallest stack of pennies they can in under a minute. Each must build their own individual stack.

The team with the highest stack combined wins the game. You may play one, or as many rounds as you wish. An excellent final activity would be to take that change, along with other donations, and earmark it for a local charity. You may also choose to use this activity to kick off a week-long team challenge, encouraging each team to collect change within the school and community. This additional challenge could be a great way to give back to a favorite local charity.

Cookie Monster — Again, divide your staff into teams. Choose one team member from each group to participate. Purchase firm cookies that are large in size and will not easily break apart. (No soft chocolate chip cookies, trust me #messalert.) Sit each participant in a chair next to their competitors. Have the brave participants tilt their heads back and balance the large cookie on their foreheads. Set a timer for one minute. Only using facial muscles—no hands!—the competitors must maneuver the cookie to their mouths. The team that gets the most cookies to their mouths wins! Ensure you have ample cookies available and a trash can nearby for those that hit the ground. You may play a single round or multiple rounds if you choose. This is an animated and fun activity, so get ready for the laughs.

Who Remembers Flip Cup? — This game may be familiar, minus the filthy frat house and splinters from junky plywood tables. Ahh, yes, remember those glorious days?! This version may lack alcoholic beverages, but it is equally fun and competitive. Once again, divide your staff into teams. Place your teams at separate tables; they may be rectangular, long, or even round. Most importantly, the number of members competing must be equal. You may opt for smaller teams so that participants go twice to keep the numbers even. This is a great team-building activity, so I encourage all team members to give it a go! Place one Solo cup in front of each member. Place the cup on the table properly. In an orderly fashion, each member must move the cup to the edge of the table, placing two fingers under the base, and attempt to flip the cup until it is upside down and resting on its rim. Once the first team member successfully flips the cup, the next one goes. The team that circulates through each member successfully wins. No timer is required.

Finders, Keepers — Teacher communication is key, so why not practice it? This is an exciting and physical activity that is not for the timid teacher or staff member. I suggest using a large open room or an empty gymnasium. You may direct participants to sit on the floor so they can crawl or let them use little scooters. Each team will choose one participant, who must be blindfolded. Place ten large items on the floor and set the timer for 90 seconds. Allow each group to go individually. The game rules are simple: teammates must verbally direct their blindfolded participant around the room to collect as many objects as they can in the time allowed. The team that gathers the most objects wins!

Suck It Up — There is no crying in education! We have all been in an awkward situation where a meeting did not go the way we wanted it to, or a parent phone call went awry. Suck it up, take it all in, and move on; remember that tomorrow is a new day. Okay, so here is how you play the game. You may choose to have 1–3 team members to compete at once or in rounds. Each participant will have two medium-sized bowls and a straw. Fill one bowl with M&M's and leave the other empty. Set the timer for one minute and challenge participants to move the candy from one bowl to the other using only one hand and the straw. At the end of the minute, count the M&M's to see which participant has moved the most candy. Declare them the winner! Make sure everyone gets some candy after the challenge as a sweet reward.

Paint and Sip! — Maybe it's that type of year, or it's been a crazy work week where your staff just needs to unwind. No team challenges, maybe just some team bonding. Invite your art teacher or perhaps hire a professional artist to walk your staff through creating a simple yet beautiful piece of artwork. Provide staff with delicious cheese, crackers, and seltzers galore! Play some relaxing music; make your co-workers feel appreciated and special.

Stack 25 — Choose 1–3 members to compete at once. No timer is needed. For each participant, stack 24 red Solo cups in a pyramid on a table. On the top, place an alternative-colored cup, or simply color the rim or the cup with a sharpie to make it stand out. Allowing participants only to use one hand and the tabletop, their challenge is to move the colored cup to the bottom of the cup pyramid and work it back at the top. The first participant to get that colored cup back up to the top wins!

Flip the Tablecloth — Here is an oldie but goodie. Sneakers or flats are highly recommended; we want to build teamwork, not stress our school nurses with injury reports. First, head to a local dollar store and purchase heavily lined tablecloths. These must be sturdy and preferably plastic so that they can survive some wear and tear. I recommend making teams no larger than four and separating them in an open space, such as a gymnasium floor or a spacious classroom. Challenge each team to stand as a group on their opened tablecloths. Once you say start, the team must work together while only using their feet (no hands or outside helpers) to flip that tablecloth without stepping off the fabric. Once the tablecloth is flipped and spread out perfectly, the challenge is complete. The team that completes this challenge first wins.

Tower Power — I always dreamed of traveling to Dubai and seeing some of the tallest and most cleverly designed buildings in the world. For now, this team challenge will have to fill that void. On a positive note, this challenge is "all hands on deck!" All team members can work at once while the timer counts down five minutes.

Here is what you need and how to play: Each team will need a large table, flat floor, or other working space; they will be supplied with a large stack of basic Styrofoam plates and cups. These are the building supplies. The sky's the limit, and whatever team constructs the tallest tower using some, all, or any variation of the supplies wins!

Find Your Other Half — Teachers tend to bond quickly, find someone they can vent to, eat lunch with, and maybe shop or grab a quick beverage with after the bell. Some even refer to this person as their work wife or work husband. Regardless of their nicknames, these dynamic duos exist in every school. It is important to encourage opportunities for teachers and staff to meet new or different members from their buildings.

This simple and fun activity can encourage staff to mix and mingle with new people and step out of their comfort zone. So here is how you play "Find Your Other Half"! Prior to the staff meeting, place random index cards in sealed envelopes inside each staff member's mailbox. Ask them to bring the envelope to the meeting, and no peeking! Once the meeting starts, ask the staff to break the seal and remove the card. Each card will have a random word written on it. Staff cannot read the word out loud or share it with anyone else in the room. Ask each staff member to randomly choose a person in the meeting and tape that index card to their back. At this point, every staff should have an index card taped to their back with a word they don't know on it. Now here is where it gets exciting. Challenge the staff to walk around the room and ask only yes and no questions to find out the word written on their card.

Each player may only ask three questions before moving on to the next staff member. Their mission is to find out what the word on their back is! Once they are sure, they must "find their other half." For example, if you have "peanut butter," you may be looking for your soulmate, "jelly." If you have "snow," you'd better find "flake." This is more challenging than you might think and really can generate some laughs.

Mini Stack Attack — Think as if you are building a replica of the Pyramids of Giza, but cooler! Here is the challenge: hand your teachers 36 tiny but sturdy cups. The ones I recommend you use are small mouthwash rinse paper cups, but any shot glass-size cup will do. No timer is needed. The first staff member who stacks the cups into a pyramid, preferably in one line, and unstacks them, placing all 36 back in a single stack, wins!

For example, to successfully build the pyramid structure, the bottom row needs to consist of 8 cups, the second row 7, the third row 6...you get the idea. You may want to show an image, construct a pyramid of your own, or just let the teams figure it out. The choice is yours. You may play this game once or do rounds. This is a simple, inexpensive, and fun challenge. Be creative and enjoy the chaos.

Escape Room — Every school has one or two staff members who are incredibly talented in escaping the building, especially right after the bell! You may want to recruit them for this next team challenge! This challenge will take time to create and execute. If you're a creative and hands-on administrator or teacher, this might be an exciting one to participate in.

Have your staff divide up into teams and place them at tables located in different areas of the room. Make sure the tables are spaced out so that they don't hear each other. I recommend placing an oversized cardboard key in a locked box and placing this on display at the front of your meeting room. Explain to your teams that the doors to the room are locked, and in order to leave, they must solve the puzzles to reveal the code on the lock! You will need a lock with multiple numeric scrolls on the exterior. This lock should be placed on the box that the fake key is located in.

Each team will be provided with a large manila envelope with the words "TOP SECRET" stamped on the exterior. Challenge the teams to solve the riddles in the packet that will eventually lead them to the correct numeric code on the lock. The first team to "escape" wins! I highly recommend that each team receive the exact same puzzles in the spirit of fairness. I also recommend that these puzzles require different skills to engage the entire team.

The Leaning Tower of Awesome — Bigger is not always better, but it is for this whole-team challenge! Gather your teams and place them at large tables. Each team will receive one box of spaghetti and one bag of minia-ture marshmallows. I highly recommend playing some authentic Italian music in the background and possibly serving some sparkling water! Once the teams are separated and spaced out with their supplies, challenge them to construct the tallest spaghetti tower. This activity is a full team challenge, so every member can roll up their sleeves and participate. You may choose the amount of time allowed for your challengers to build. I recommend a minimum of 10 minutes and a maximum of 30, or you can extend this time if you provide cappuccinos and espressos. Just a thought!

Olympic Obstacle Course — This is not for the faint of heart! This after-school physical challenge will require you to collaborate with your PE staff and maybe even a few dedicated custodians. With an Olympic theme, develop head-to-head obstacle course races to determine which team is truly the best. You may want to design your races to suit your gymnasium equipment, and you might even charge admission to spectators and donate the proceeds to a local charity. Opening ceremonies and handmade flags would be creative bonuses. Just don't forget to make a special station for your nurse or school trainer, just in case. If things go not as expected, maybe give this one another shot in four years.

Important Dates to Celebrate

SEPTEMBER

- National IT Professionals Day takes place on the third Tuesday of September. Check your search engine for yearly dates.

OCTOBER

- National Custodians Day, October 2nd

- National Coaches Day, October 6th

- Boss's Day, October 16th

NOVEMBER

- National Substitute Teacher Appreciation Day, November 20th

- Parent Teacher Appreciation Day (PTA) — Pick any date you wish, but a day in November might be a perfect choice

JANUARY

- School Resource Officer's Day falls around January 9th

FEBRUARY

- National School Counseling Week is celebrated the first week of February.

APRIL

- Paraprofessional Appreciation Day, April 1st. Recognizes paraprofessional educators for their contributions in our schools.

- National School Librarian Day, April 4th

- National Assistant Principal Day falls on the second week in April

- Administrative Professionals Day, anywhere from April 21st to 27th, varying year to year

- School Bus Drivers Appreciation Day falls around April 27th. This day may vary by state each year, so check your search engines for yearly updates

MAY

- Principal's Day, May 1st (Some prefer to celebrate "Boss's Day" in October to separate it from Teacher Appreciation Week)

- School Nutrition Employee Week falls around the first week in May

- Teacher Appreciation Week is observed during the first full week of May each year. "National Teacher Day" falls on the Tuesday of Teacher Appreciation Week

- National School Nurses Day takes place around the second week of May. This day tends to fluctuate

NOTE: Always refer to your search engine for yearly calendar updates and newly introduced celebrations.

How to Build an Awesome Year

(An Activities-at-a-Glance Calendar)

● ● ●

"TO BUILD A HAPPY AND HEALTHY SCHOOL WITHOUT A PLAN IS JUST A WISH"

A school filled with joyous staff members that feel valued and respected will transfer that same love and gratitude to their students tenfold! The excitement you generate for your teachers and staff will simply roll over into the classrooms and community. This is why it's so important for schools to be inspirational and appealing places to work. When teachers are having fun, their students will share that same excitement. A school with a positive culture is something that everyone wants to be part of. Regardless of whether your school is awesome to work at (or not!), generating new ideas to raise morale or simply switching things up will benefit any workplace. Here is a sample school year with tons of ideas and motivational, morale-boosting activities. Each month has several options to choose from. Remember, though; it is crucial to limit monthly activities and change them from year to year. Keep your choices fresh and choose only a few each month, so your staff is not overwhelmed with excitement.

August / September

- To Theme or Not to Theme — send out a survey with a list of ideas and get staff to help you pick a school theme that will carry throughout the year. Having a part in the process will mean more staff are likely to participate.

- Celebrate "Summer Milestones" — share with your staff news about newlyweds, tenure achievements, graduations, births, new pets, engagements, new homes, and so on among building staff. Place these announcements in your back-to-school staff newsletter, make a digital announcement card, or simply share the great news during your faculty "welcome back to school" meeting.

- Select staff/teacher teams, and commemorate them by inspiring each to create team flags or choosing a unique team name. Encourage these teams to work together throughout the year while competing in building challenges.

- Contact your local PTA and small businesses and request donations, such as $5 gift cards or small items. Look for packaged cookies, candy, treats, or coffee vouchers to local cafés. These will come in handy for using as prizes throughout the year, so stock up!

- Make the first day back extra special. Host a back-to-school brunch, or create a photo booth for teachers and place it in the lounge! Save these festive pictures for a last-day photo op in June and do a side-by-side comparison. Proudly hang these photos in your teacher's lounge. Remember always to celebrate the fun moments.

- Incorporate your school theme into daily activities as much as you can! Trim the entryway, cafeteria, or even the library with decorations complementing your theme. Use this theme in your parent newsletters and tweets. Host a staff dress-up day for theme-inspired costumes. Challenge teachers to a school-themed door decorating or bulletin board contest. Don't forget to award prizes or certificates of recognition!

- First Day of School Dance Party! Shake your pom-poms, clap those hands, get the blood pumping, and celebrate. Host a dance party as your students enter the building on the first day. Have fun and incorporate your theme whenever possible.

- Make Back-to-School Night extra special. Supply staff with unity pins or corsages during your evening's festivities. Leave snacks in the teacher's lounge, with a message to the effect of, "Meet and Greet, Here's Something Sweet," because your staff will need a pick-me-up during this extra-long workday. Show them you care by allowing for a dress-down day before they must change into something fancy prior to parents arriving.

- Download a digital spinning wheel and import your staff members' names into it. There are multiple free online spinning tools to assist when awarding random staff giveaways. They are exciting to watch and will make the first five minutes of any staff meeting thrilling.

- Award prizes often. September prizes can be awarded for door decor contests, best-decorated classroom, best first-day attire, or staff member who worked the most volunteer summer hours setting up, to name a few.

- September is go time! It is a time of significant transition for many. If your faculty meetings allow some downtime between training sessions, give that time back to your staff. Allow them the freedom to work independently back in their classrooms. This will help lower anxiety levels.

- Make "Teacher's Lounge Seat Sacks." What staff lounge doesn't need some extra storage? These simple-to-sew chair covers will give your staff a place to stow their reading materials or laptops. Your lounge will be decluttered and filled with Zen.

- Host a "Bites and Bytes" party during IT Personnel Appreciation Day. Grab a cake with a big "Thank You" written on it to show your IT staff appreciation for keeping you up and running digitally all year.

October

- "Wurst." Faculty meeting. Ever. Theme one of your October faulty meetings around Oktoberfest! Supply staff with pretzels and mustard to snack on. Pass out some cold root beers and play some authentic German music in the background. A super fun principal may even pull up their socks when reviewing the agenda.

- "Our School Sparkles Because of You." Celebrate your custodians by treating them to a catered lunch, and show them how much you care by lining your halls with handwritten thank-you notes from teachers, students, staff, and administrators.

- Do some building-wide beautification. Get outdoors with your colleagues and plant some bulbs. This is an excellent opportunity for bonding and team-building. When the flowers bloom in spring, they are a wonderful reminder of your work family blooming throughout the year.

- Create a "Boo Bucket" by filling a Halloween-themed container with classroom supplies and surprise a coworker with it and an anonymous note of appreciation. Encourage them to pay it forward. Start this in early October so that the bucket travels throughout the building during the month.

- Assign staff a secret buddy. Promote a morale-boosting activity where teachers can decorate mini pumpkins with an encouraging message or write complementary notes to a fellow staff member. Participants can slip the pumpkins inside their buddy's mailbox or place them on their desk when no one is looking.

- Add some excitement to that faculty meeting closest to Halloween. Challenge your teachers to a "Wrap a Mummy" team challenge. Provide your staff with some toilet paper, allow them to pick a brave team member, and kick-off that meeting with some good old competition and laughter. Play some Halloween music and take some memorable pictures for the yearbook staff page.

- If you are a principal or athletic director, make sure you give a shout-out to your dedicated coaches! Create an e-card or picture collage to share with your community honoring their years of dedicated service.

- Decorate a portable food cart with fun fall decor. Create a sign for it saying, "Orange you Glad you Work Here" on the front. With a Sharpie, draw pumpkin faces on some oranges and clementines to make your treats extra special. Stop by each classroom and offer a healthy treat to your deserving staff.

- Host a "Murder Mystery" team-building activity during your staff meeting. Assemble your teachers in their designated teams and challenge them to solve various puzzles to find out "who done it!" If the victim is the principal, remember, it could be anyone!

- Make "Witches Brew" recipe books. Collect delicious soup recipes from staff members and create photocopied recipe books to pass out. This is a fun way for your cooking-inspired staff to contribute to building positive morale.

- Award prizes to teams and individuals for costume ideas during Halloween. Maybe even encourage your staff members to incorporate the theme for extra points.

November

November is one of the shortest months in education due to teachers' conventions, conferences, and holidays. Try to limit activities.

- This is a great month to dedicate a day to show appreciation for your PTA. This month is filled with conferences, so many parents will be present inside your building. Some ideas include: letters from students displayed in the halls showing their appreciation. Teachers may choose to create a thank-you banner and place it at your building entrance, allowing students to sign it or put a personal message on it. Highlight PTA volunteers throughout the month on Twitter, and maybe even shoot a video of some little ones singing a song to express their gratitude. Share that video with complimentary homemade cookies at the next PTA meeting. Give them the same love they regularly show to your staff and students throughout the year. Kindness is contagious!

- Hide the Turkey. Hide a large, colorful laminated "Turkey" somewhere in your building. Challenge staff to find the hidden gobbler, and they can claim a prize!

- Head to your local wholesale store and grab a few apple and/or pumpkin pies! Decorate your food cart with some fancy fall decor and a large sign that reads, "I Only Have Pies for You." Deliver these slices to your staff as you visit each room. Don't forget the plates, forks, and napkins!

- Introduce the digital spinner to your staff. To maximize time for your staff during meetings, you could do a quick icebreaker by playing the digital spinning game. Award your winner with a "Free Get Out of Duty" pass.

- National Substitute Teacher Appreciation Day is at the end of November. If you have special "regular" substitute teachers and would like to recognize their efforts, handwrite a note to them expressing your gratitude. For giggles and some extra love, place a hoagie or sub shop gift card in the envelope too.

- November is all about "Giving Thanks:" design a staff shout-out bulletin board and place it in the teacher's lounge. Encourage staff to write heartfelt notes of gratitude to one another.

- Start a Staff Food Drive. Provide staff with a "Free Dress-Down Day" when they bring in non-perishable food items to be donated to your local community food pantry. When your staff focuses on the good, they tend to shine!

- Fall Festival Potluck. Encourage staff to bring in some delicious soups or fall favorites to enjoy on a brisk autumn day. Remember, it's always nice to decorate your teacher's lounge and encourage staff bonding activities throughout the year.

December

- Host a "Winter Wonderland" decorating contest. Place teachers in their teams or simply challenge them by grade level. Teachers can choose an area of their hallway to decorate elaborately. Snap some pictures and allow the community to vote on the best winter wonderland decor.

- Shake things up at your next faculty meeting by participating in a physical challenge. Challenge your teams to a wrap attack! Wrap multiple boxes with holiday wrapping paper and place them inside additional wrapped boxes. I suggest repeating this method until you have nested five boxes, with the final one containing a Hershey's Kiss. Each team is to choose one team member to compete. Place oven mitts on all participants' hands and watch them struggle to work their way down to the final box. No physical challenge is complete without a prize. Pass out a one-day VIP Parking Pass to each winning team member. Remember to hand out bags of Hershey's Kisses to all the staff!

- Ugly Holiday Sweater Day. This one is popular in schools across the country. On this particular day, add some additional cheer! Challenge your teams to create a digital holiday or Christmas card. Post your final card images in the cafeteria and let your students vote for their favorite photo. Share your staff's creativity and love for the holidays with your community or make one giant school holiday card to post on your webpage.

- Who doesn't like hot cocoa? Put a winter wonderland spin on your food cart and treat your staff to some delicious hot chocolate. Don't forget the marshmallows! A super staff member or administrator would hand-deliver these cups in a seventies-inspired ski outfit or elf costume—but no pressure.

- Holiday Bake-Off Bliss. Deck the halls with sugar and sweets. Suggest a holiday treat day. Enlist teachers to bring in their go-to holiday favorites during lunch. Transform the meeting room into a winter wonderland, even project some December movie classics on the wall. Set up a cute photo booth in the corner and watch their faces glow.

- Build a Reindeer physical challenge. This activity will include all team members, and it's pretty much laugh-out-loud hysterical. Save this for a rainy day when everyone needs a good chuckle. Place each team at a table and supply them with 1 pair of pantyhose, 15 red or green balloons, a small red paper circle, and a glue stick. Have each team select an exceptionally "outgoing" member to dress up. Set the timer for three minutes and challenge them "build the reindeer" by blowing up the balloons and stuffing them into the pantyhose legs until they're full, then placing them on the participant's head with a cherry-red nose to top off the look. The team with the best reindeer "look" wins the challenge. Award all your spirited reindeer with coffee gift cards for being great sports!

- Mix things up. Switch up your traditional holiday staff party; maybe consider hosting it at a bowling alley instead. Always make each year a little different and unique.

- Appreciate your staff with some homemade baked goods and a handwritten card. Show them you care, especially during the holiday season.

- Put up a large "Tree of Thanks" made of paper in your staff lounge. After winter break, things get exhausting and tiresome fast. Encourage staff to write anonymous thank-you notes and post them on green paper leaves you've provided. This tree should blossom by June.

January

- Surprise your staff with some New Year's glasses/hats to wear on the first day back. Head to your local dollar store, or simply collect and recycle some New Year's Eve items at the party you just attended. Stuff their mailboxes and encourage them to have a little fun with their students.

- Place witty, printable New Year's Resolution Mad Libs on teachers' desks with a warm "welcome back" greeting. These are fun for staff to fill out during their leisure time.

- We're Off to a Sweet Year! Provide your staff with healthy treats in the teacher's lounge, such as fruit or apple crisps.

- Participate in the "Snowball Fight" icebreaker activity at your January faculty meeting. I described this earlier in the book—reference the Icebreaker Warm-up chapter for details about this activity.

- School Resource Officer's Day falls around January 9th. Celebrate their dedication to your staff and students by presenting them with hand-made cards from your students and maybe a cup of joe. Have some fun in the teacher's lounge by setting up a "cop" corn machine with bags teachers can fill.

- January is about getting a fresh start and focusing on staff health and wellness. This might be a great time to have a nutritionist visit your next faculty meeting or to cancel it altogether and treat your teachers to an aerobic activity, even simply a pleasant stroll around the neighborhood (if weather permits).

- Create a Staff Health and Wellness Board in the teacher's lounge. Inspire staff to post wellness-related articles and healthy recipes.

- Challenge your teachers to a 30-day self-care challenge. Pass out a calendar for the month of January filled with little daily wellness challenges. These can be found online for free, or you and your wellness committee can create an original calendar to fit your staff's needs. For example, Day 1: Consume a vegetable with every meal. Day 2: Go on a 10-minute walk. These daily challenges can motivate your coworkers to get back on track.

- If hiring a massage therapist for a day is not in your yearly budget, invest in a portable massage chair. These relatively inexpensive mini machines would be a great addition to any staff wellness room or faculty lounge. Reserve one or two chairs near an outlet and let staff utilize them throughout the year.

- Play "Hide the Snowman." The lucky staff member who finds the Snowman wins a yoga mat.

February

- Host a Super Bowl-Themed Luncheon. Invite staff to contribute some of their favorite tailgating entrees and desserts. Toss in a free dress-down day and encourage colleagues to wear their favorite sports jerseys. This is also a great time to donate canned goods to your local food pantry! In the Super Bowl spirit, place a large table outside the teacher's lounge with the participating teams' logos on each side. Have staff root for their favorite team by placing a canned good on that team's side of the table. Let's see who the building's favorite team is!

- Remember to thank your fantastic guidance counselors this month! National School Counseling Week is celebrated the first week of February. Make them feel special by mentioning them on social media, and who knows, maybe host a "Donut Forget Our Counselors Rock" doughnut breakfast. Make sure you include your social workers too! Individuals who offer counseling to our youth are dedicated to their craft, and they provide students with valuable resources. Make sure you show them you care.

- "Send a Hug in a Mug" activity. Promote positivity as staff participates, and "pay it forward" by filling and decorating mugs to send to a colleague as a surprise. Free downloads and directions can be found on Teacherspayteachers.com under "You've Been Mugged."

- Place "You are the BALM! Happy Valentine's Day" cards with ChapStick attached in each staff member's mailbox. Countless creative graphics for this concept can be found online.

- Give them a giggle and a sweet treat too! Decorate your food cart this month with some conversation hearts, Valentine's logos, and yes, bananas. For this month, use the sign: "I'm Bananas For You." Treat your staff to a healthy banana, and maybe a piece of chocolate too. Like always, you must hand-deliver these items and make sure you thank them for their contributions throughout the year.

- Play "Put a Ring on It." Theme your faculty meeting with some Valentine's Day love and get your staff on their feet. You may want to play some Beyoncé in the background for some inspiration.

- Have staff teams assemble and get each to choose two lucky competitors. In the center of the room, roughly 10–12 feet away, place a large cone. Each player will have two turns to toss their hoops over the cone. The team that lands the most successful tosses wins! Award them some points or simply give their team a giant bag of Ring Pops.

- Assemble a "You Break My Heart" edible bulletin board in your teacher's lounge: tape red paper napkins over paper cups with hidden treats, such as mini chocolate bars or Hershey's Kisses, inside. When a staff member needs a quick pick-me-up, they can punch a cup and scoop up a sweet prize.

March

March is a very long month with no real breaks due to the educational calendar. This month feels like the last few miles of a marathon for teachers, staff assistants, and building administrators. The finish line is in sight, but it is tough to keep pushing through the pain as your legs and body start to break down. Educators are exhausted at this point, with state testing dates looming around the corner. So remember to focus on their wellness and try to keep things light.

- Show your staff some love this March by setting up a mini-wellness table in your teacher's lounge. Place stress-releasing activities and handouts there. Some items may include: mandala coloring sheets, stress balls, coupons to a nearby spa, bubble wrap for popping and don't forget some mindful comedic quotes.

- "Thank You a Latte" coffee cart. Don't forget the double espresso for your staff who will need an extra boost this month. Provide teachers and paraprofessionals with a fresh cup of coffee to keep their spirits high.

- Establish multiple dress-up opportunities and door decorating contests during this month, especially if your school celebrates "Read Across America" week. Assist with your yearly festivities by providing prizes for incentives! Some great ideas include lottery tickets, candy, or free in-school vouchers (discussed in an earlier chapter). Provide your costume winner(s) with a unique surprise. You may choose to make a top costume winner for each year and invest in a plaque for your entranceway.

- Play "Catch the Rainbow" with your staff. Print 10–15 large rainbows, and with a Sharpie number, each of them on the back. Place your rainbows in hidden areas throughout your building. Hide them high, low, under chairs, in bathroom stalls—keep your staff on their toes. Explain that if a staff member finds one, he/she may return it to the main office for a "magical prize." Create prize boxes containing candy bars, bags of Skittles, or even lotto scratch-tickets, but make sure they too are numbered. Just like a tricky tray, staff can have some added fun matching the rainbows to the prizes.

- Keep your faculty meetings short and sweet. Due to the length of this month and the stress of state testing looming, keep the activities light and provide your staff some time to chat with their colleagues. Sweeten the experience by baking some treats or cookies for the meeting.

- Host a "March Madness Shootout" with your staff. Challenge them to a mean game of knockout or HORSE. Give them several opportunities this month to relieve stress and recharge their batteries.

- Host a St. Patty's-themed luncheon. Encourage coworkers to bring in their favorite green treats and entrees. There are several free printable options online if you decide to set up a photo booth. If you have an extra blender lying around, you could make "Shamrock Shakes."

April

There are many different staff members to celebrate this month:

- Paraprofessional Appreciation Day, April 1st

- National School Librarian Day, April 4th

- National Assistant Principal Day, 2nd week in April

- Administrative Professionals' Day around April 21st

- School Bus Drivers Appreciation Day, which takes place April 27th (depending on your state)

During this busy time, you may want to join forces with your sunshine club and/or your PTA to make sure all your special coworkers are recognized. Some ideas include decorating their classroom or office doors or providing them with gift baskets, flowers, or balloons. Or simply offer them a handwritten note of appreciation. Remember to recognize them in your monthly bulletins. Make them feel appreciated and special!

- If you host school competitions this month, make sure you award your staff booby prizes. Keep up with some April Fools' Day Fun.

- April Fools' Day Wars! Challenge your staff teams to play pranks on their competition. Award points for the most creative team prank. Ensure they snap pics of their "good" deeds and share them with your staff at the next faculty meeting for some added laughs. Be sure to play along, even if you're an administrator.

- Start off that next faculty meeting with an Easter egg hunt! Put candy, dress-down tickets, sleep-in passes, and the like inside large plastic eggs. Let your staff run wild as they track down your hidden surprises.

- Request each of your teams to brainstorm and vote for their favorite morale-building quote. They may choose a well-known inspirational quote or create their own. Send your teams out to print and/or inscribe the quote in an area of their choice.

- Relax your colleagues this month by providing service animals at the next staff meeting or during their preps to help them wind down and visit with some furry friends.

- Encourage your staff to take a break from the regular staff meetings and enjoy the outdoors. You may recommend they take a pleasant stroll around the campus or perhaps start weeding and freshening up the planting soil.

- Get ready to saddle up and host a Kentucky Derby-themed luncheon. Dress up in your most dapper attire, and don't forget to provide your staff with some non-alcoholic mint juleps! Large hats and finger foods are a must! For a bonus, you may want to have each team pick a horse and place some bets.

May

- In my experience, parents and PTA members often go above and beyond creating unique and exciting events to celebrate Teacher Appreciation Week. Give them your attention, listen to their ideas, and provide them any assistance if it is requested. There are multiple staff to recognize this month, including Principal's Day on May 1st, School Nutrition Employee Week, Teacher Appreciation Week, and National School Nurses Day.

- Nacho Average Staff Meeting. Surprise your staff this month with some delicious nachos, and who knows; you may want to even toss in a piñata for some extra pizazz. There will be many sweets in the teacher's lounge due to Teacher Appreciation Day, so this is a nice twist!

- Get outside as much as you can. If you are hosting a professional development meeting, encourage your staff to take outdoor breaks between sessions. This is an excellent time of year to get outside and plant some flowers and shrubs. Your building will look great for June's outdoor graduation or end-of-year festivities.

- It's Grill Time. Rent a professional grill and cook up some hotdogs and hamburgers for your staff. Invite your colleagues to bring the paper plates, utensils, and delicious sides to share. Consider laying out some blankets to make it a picnic. The possibilities are endless.

- April showers brought May flowers. Place bundles of fresh-cut local flowers in your staff restroom with an encouraging message.

- National Paper Airplane Day takes place this month. Spice up your faculty meeting by challenging each team to design and toss a paper plane. You can set up a large hula hoop at one end of the room and award points to groups that can successfully navigate through the hoop with their personally designed plane.

- Build a "Fresh Start Cart." Provide your staff with some mini boxes of cereal, a simple piece of fruit, or a sweet breakfast pop tart. The days will seem longer this month as teachers and staff prepare for the home stretch. Raise their spirits in the early hours of the day.

June

- Awards, Prizes for Teams, and Trophies. Make sure you customize your certificates and plan a lovely ceremony for your colleagues! Dedicate an entire staff meeting to reflect upon your building's achieved goals and overall accomplishments! Make your staff feel special, and make sure they are enjoying this time. I strongly suggest holding this meeting in early June, since this month is action-packed, and you absolutely want to make staff feel recognized and appreciated for all the work they put in this year.

- Waffles Anyone? Why not switch it up? "Exhale stress, Inhale Waffles." This is a simple and inexpensive breakfast option. In the middle of a long table, place 2–4 toasters with bowls of frozen waffles and plastic tongs around them. Add decorative plates, napkins, and some specialty toppings, and voila!

- Dress Down, Morale Up! During the last few days, your staff will be cleaning, packing, storing, and potentially moving. Toss in some extra dress-down days so they are comfortable.

- Let There Be Cake! It's always nice to provide a large sheet cake for the staff at the end of the year! If you went with a school theme, make sure the cake matches to follow the building theme to the very end.

- One Last Spin. It may be worth saving your big-ticket items for the very end. Surprise your staff with some super giveaways: "Room Painted Over the Summer," "Cricket," "A new staff laptop," "Large Gift Basket of School Supplies," Multiple Gift Cards." Remember to make this final celebration grand!

- Ice Cream Makes Everything Better. This may be a stretch, but explore the possibilities of having a truck arrive at your building after school.

- End the year with a good laugh. A fun staff giveaway is a "Summer Emergency Kit." Be creative and have fun assembling them. In small plastic bags, place fun tickets with statements like "Sleep in till noon" or "No Bus Duty the whole month of July." Add some candy and a few relaxing bags of tea. Maybe even toss in a bag of Skinny Pop since it's bathing suit season. Put your own twist on them and make them comical.

- Host an End of the Year Get-Together! Have your sunshine committee choose a location and possibly a theme to match (Luau, the 80s, Masks & Mimosas). Once that last bus pulls out of the parking lot, make sure you and your staff celebrate teacher style!

- Lastly, send out a survey. At the end of each year, ask for feedback from your colleagues. Make these surveys anonymous so people feel safe to be totally honest. Find out what icebreakers, activities, games, and food options they loved or disliked, and so on. Also, if you are theming, allow them to vote and choose the following year's theme. This would be beneficial for staff to brainstorm and prepare over the summer, for as one year ends, the next begins!

In Closing

I would like to express my deepest gratitude that the ideas and methods outlined in this book will flow through the reader to enact positive change within their schools. I am excited about those who wish to build energizing, positive, and loving learning environments for all to thrive in. After all, happy teachers make joyous and prosperous students. I would like to thank the numerous devoted and passion-filled teachers who inspired me to become the person I am today. I have been blessed along my journey in education to have witnessed great enthusiasm and talent. Special thanks to two extraordinary schools filled with some of the most devoted and innovative educators ever known: Liberty Elementary School and Birchwood Elementary School. Now Go..... Make Your School Awesome!